MY RELATIONS WITH CARLYLE

MY RELATIONS WITH CARLYLE

BY

JAMES ANTHONY FROUDE

*TOGETHER WITH A LETTER FROM THE LATE
SIR JAMES STEPHEN, BART., K.C.S.I.
DATED DECEMBER 9, 1886*

 BOOKS FOR LIBRARIES PRESS
FREEPORT, NEW YORK

First Published 1903
Reprinted 1971

INTERNATIONAL STANDARD BOOK NUMBER:
0-8369-5766-0

LIBRARY OF CONGRESS CATALOG CARD NUMBER:
70-154150

PRINTED IN THE UNITED STATES OF AMERICA

PREFATORY NOTE

In making facts public on which Mr. Froude had, after long and anxious consideration, decided to be silent, we are fully aware of the responsibility we are taking on ourselves. For the re-opening of the controversy, however, we are not to blame. The following private account, written by Mr. Froude himself, of his own relations with Mr. Carlyle would never have been given to the world had not the production of the 'New Letters and Memorials of Jane Welsh Carlyle,' with the serious charges contained in the Introduction and Footnotes, appeared to us to demand its publication.

In the face of such charges, we feel that we should not be doing our duty as Mr. Froude's representatives if we failed to use the means which we possess of vindicating his memory. It seems to us best that Mr. Froude should speak in his own words, even though they may not be those which he himself might finally have chosen, had he been now living, and had he consented at last to speak in his own defence.

The history of the Notes is given on a subsequent page. As the style itself shows, they have received no literary revision; and none has been attempted by ourselves. We have corrected a few clerical errors; we have omitted a few passages, containing intimate reflections and recollections, unconnected with the point at issue; and two passages, dealing not with Mr. Carlyle but with certain business complications which arose out of the publication of his Memoirs, we have transferred *in extenso* to the Appendix.

With the Notes we publish, by permission of Sir Herbert Stephen, a letter from Sir James Stephen to Mr. Froude, which was printed in 1886 for private circulation only, and in which reference is made to the above business matter. The letter is evidence which cannot be disputed as to Sir James Stephen's opinion of his co-executor's conduct, throughout a difficult and most painful business, and it shows incidentally the complications which resulted from Mr. Carlyle's changes of purpose.

ASHLEY A. FROUDE.
MARGARET FROUDE.

May 22, 1903.

MY RELATIONS WITH CARLYLE.

Mr. Froude's account of his 'Relations with Carlyle' was found after his death in a despatch-box with a copy of Mr. Carlyle's will and a few business papers. The notes are written in pencil in a note-book, and, so far as is known, Mr. Froude had shown them to no one. The first few pages are of too intimate a nature to be given to the public; but they are painful evidence of how acutely Mr. Froude had suffered under the criticism to which he refused to reply. The short account which he gives of his own early life, is only important because of the light thrown by it upon his first acquaintance with Mr. Carlyle. He describes how he had been bred up in the usual way, had gone to school and college, passed fairly through his university career, and in process of time gained a fellowship, the natural result of which had been ordination. He had taken deacon's orders, and looked to the Church as his regular profession. So much as a doubt, he tells us, had so far never crossed his mind of the truth of the creed in which he had been brought up.

'It was at this time,' he says, 'that Carlyle's books came in my way. They produced on me what Evangelicals call "a conviction of sin." They taught me the intense seriousness of life; the inevitable consequence, in the injury to the moral nature, of every careless wrong act, which no repentance could completely remedy. For the first time I was made to realise the meaning of duty and the overpowering obligation to do it. But, along with this, Carlyle's books taught me that the religion in which I had been reared was but one of many dresses in which spiritual truth had arrayed itself, and that the creed was not literally true so far as it was a narrative of facts.'

Under this influence he gave up his fellowship and abandoned his orders, feeling that the change which was taking place in his own belief made it impossible for him honestly to adopt the career designed for him. In taking this step he compromised all his earthly prospects. His father was severely displeased, and refused to do any more for him. He was turned adrift upon the world to struggle as he might, and as the law then stood every profession was closed to him. The period of struggle in his case did not last long; within a few years Mr. Froude had made a position for himself; but while it lasted it was hard, and he had voluntarily embarked upon it. This crisis in his life was due to Mr. Carlyle's influence. 'I mention it,' he says, 'to show how little likely it is that for any motive of my own I *should have wilfully misrepresented his character when it came to me to tell what that character was. I had every conceivable motive, spiritual and earthly, to show him in the most favourable of all possible lights, with nothing on the other side save the sense which he had himself impressed upon me, that, under all hazards to oneself and under all circumstances, it was necessary to stick to the truth.*'

The narrative can now be continued in Mr. Froude's own words :

I was introduced to Carlyle soon after I left the University. I saw him from time to time, not often, for I lived far off in the country. He was very good to me. He helped me when he could. I became intimate to some extent with Mrs. Carlyle, with whom I occasionally corresponded. She liked me, I believe, at least, so Carlyle told me, while I thought her the most brilliant and interesting woman that I had ever fallen in with; so much thought, so much lightness and brilliancy, such sparkling scorn and tenderness combined, I had never met with together in any human being. It was evident that she was suffering; she was always in indifferent health, she had no natural cheerfulness, at least, none when I knew her. Rumour said that she and Carlyle quarrelled often, and I could easily believe it from occasional expressions about him which fell from her. But it was clear, too, that she greatly admired him. Various hints were dropped in the circle which gathered at the house in Cheyne Row, about the nature of the relations between them, that their marriage was not a real marriage, and was only companionship, &c. I paid no attention to a matter which was no business of mine. I have never been curious about family secrets, and have always as a rule of my life declined to listen to communications which were no business of mine. It was enough for me to be admitted to the Cheyne Row tea-parties on my occasional visits, and enjoy the brilliancy of the conversation, whether it was with him or with her.

In 1860, I removed to London to live. Such acquaintance as I had with the Carlyles I hoped to keep up, but I did not expect, and for the reasons which I have mentioned I did not wish, that it should be closer than it was. Carlyle himself I admired intensely, but it was with admiration too complete for pleasant social relationship. His manner was impatient and overbearing. He denounced everybody and everything, and, though what he said was in my opinion intensely true and right, yet I felt that it would be impossible to live with him on equal terms. One loves those who are not too far removed from oneself. He seemed to me a superior order of being, whom one approached with genuine reverence, but could scarcely dare to love.

To my surprise, one evening in 1861, Carlyle called on me, expressed a wish to see more of me, invited me to come more often to his house, to be his companion in his walks and rides, &c. Nothing could be more flattering. I consented, and I was now continually in Cheyne Row. In all this the advances were on Carlyle's side. I had made no effort to press myself into his intimacy, still less into intimacy with Mrs. Carlyle. To refuse such hands when they were held out to me I thought would be ungracious and unnecessary. I felt myself highly honoured besides, and I promised myself pleasure and advantage from increased opportunities of quiet conversation with him. When more than one person was present he spoke in monologue, pouring out cataracts generally of denunciation against all manner of things and persons. When alone with a single companion he was delightful, brilliantly entertaining, sympathetic, and even occasionally tolerant of what at other times he would execrate, and full of the widest information about all things and subjects.

Introduced thus into closer relations with the life at Cheyne Row, I could not help becoming acquainted with many things which I would rather not have known. If Carlyle was busy he was in his sound-proof room and never allowed himself to be interrupted. Any one who disturbed him at such times was not likely to repeat the experiment. Mrs.

Carlyle was very much alone. She was in bad health and he did not seem to see it, or if he did, he forgot it immediately in the multitude of thoughts which pressed upon him. She rarely saw him except at meal-times. She sat by herself in her drawing-room, either reading or entertaining visitors who bored her, and of whom she dared not ask him to relieve her. She suffered frightfully from neuralgia, which she bore with more than stoical endurance, but it was evident that her life was painful and dreary. She was sarcastic when she spoke of her husband—a curious blending of pity, contempt, and other feelings. One had heard of violent quarrels from others who were admitted within the circle, and one began to realise that they might perhaps be true. One had heard that she had often thought of leaving Carlyle, and as if she had a right to leave him if she pleased. To those whom she liked she was charming—bewitching, and the thought of such a person suffering as she evidently suffered, with so little sympathy bestowed upon her, and suffering through the negligence of a man whom nevertheless one admired as one's own honoured master and teacher, was exquisitely painful. He too suffered from dyspepsia and want of sleep. But whereas she was expected to bear her trouble in patience, and received homilies on the duty of submission if she spoke impatiently, he was never more eloquent than in speaking of his own crosses. He himself had really a vigorous constitution. He never had a day of serious illness. He used to walk or ride in the wildest weather and never carried so much as an umbrella. Yet I never knew him admit that he felt well. He never spoke of himself without complaint as if he was an exceptional victim of the Destinies. She was weary of hearing a tale so often repeated, the importance of which she was so well able to value. Some degree of self-restraint is expected from all of us, even when there is something real to complain of. Without it none of us could live together. In Carlyle's catalogue of his own duties, self-restraint seemed to be forgotten. She was very little alone with him. She presided at the tea-table at the small evening gatherings of his admirers in her own charming fashion. But Carlyle on these occasions did not converse. He would not allow himself to be contradicted, but poured out whole Niagaras of scorn and vituperation sometimes for hours together, and she was wearied, as she confessed, of a tale which she had heard so often and in much of which she imperfectly believed. She would herself occasionally say this. She admired his genius as much as ever. She had accepted the destructive part of his opinions like so many others, but he had failed to satisfy her that he knew where positive truth lay. He had taken from her, as she mournfully said, the creed in which she had been bred, but he had been unable to put anything in the place of it. She believed nothing. On the spiritual side of things her mind was a perfect blank; she looked into her own heart and into the world beyond her, and it was all void and desert; there was no word of consolation, no word of hope. She was so true that it was impossible for her to satisfy herself with fine phrases about the Infinite. That confidence which sustained him in his uncertainties that 'the Maker of all things would do right,' he had never succeeded in conveying to her. He believed, or thought he believed, in a special Providence. To her it was an unmeaning phrase. I suppose that his own inconsistencies interfered with the effect of his teaching. He 'recked not his own rede,' and those whose practice falls short of their theories do not seem to believe really in their theories themselves. Carlyle was impatient, irritable, strangely forgetful of others, self-occupied and bursting into violence at the smallest and absurdest provocation—evidently a most difficult and trying household companion. All this was very distressing. Mrs. Carlyle's pale, drawn, suffering face haunted me in my dreams. I set most of it down to ill-health. I did not allow my reverence and admiration for Carlyle's intellect and high moral greatness to be interfered with. I considered him an exceptional person, whose infirmities were greater than the virtues of most other persons. I suppose I considered that to be the wife of such a man was a sufficient honour in itself, and I was more distressed than interested by the bitter things which she occasionally said of him, only I felt that I could never live with such a man. Nothing would do but the most absolute submission to him of your whole being, and then you would do only indifferently.

In 1862, her health finally broke down, and there came on that strange illness of hers which doctors failed to understand, or, if they understood it, they did not venture to speak plainly. For a year she lay in agonies, her nervous system torn to tatters—sleepless, racked with pain which was unlike any pain that she had ever felt or heard of. Carlyle's wild irritability (in one of her letters at the time she described her life with him as like keeping a mad-house) had shattered her at last. The wisest of her doctors insisted as a first necessity on her separation from him, the constant agitation of his presence, and the equally constant provocation which his forgetfulness or preoccupation made incessant in spite of efforts, taking away all hope of amendment while the cause remained. She went to Hastings, to Scotland: she was all but dead. She had again and again been given up. To all inquiries there was but one answer: 'No better. No hope.' Suddenly, as if from the grave, she came back. The illness had seemed preternatural, the recovery equally so. She had been dying. She was apparently well. She came back into society. She was weak, extremely so, but in good spirits. Carlyle had been frightened into realising how ill she had really been. It had not been that he was consciously indifferent, but he was preoccupied. He made little of other people's sufferings; she had rarely complained at the worst, and was a Stoic in the sternest sense of the word. He thought more of her comfort; he gave her a carriage. He had felt to his heart what her loss would have been to him. Those last eighteen months, he often told me, were the happiest in his married life, since the first year of it. She, too, seemed to feel more for him; not entirely as he perhaps thought, for she was unforgiving, and she had more to forgive than any one knew, but the atmosphere in Cheyne Row had cleared a little. She still mocked to me at times about him, and the resentment was there, though it showed itself less. In the midst of the improvement, and when he was absent as Lord Rector at Edinburgh, she suddenly died in her carriage. The injury had gone too deep. There had been no real amendment. Her nerves had been so shaken by her many years of suffering that some singular disease had developed itself, I believe, in her spine. At any rate, she went out one afternoon to drive round Hyde Park. I was to have been with her in the evening at tea. She had had a shock at some injury to her dog, and died without a word or a struggle.

Such an end was tragically in keeping with her singular character and history. I have spoken elsewhere of Carlyle's misery. He shut himself up in the house with her diaries and papers, and for the first time was compelled to look himself in the face, and to see what his faults had been. The worst of those faults I have concealed hitherto. I can conceal them no longer. He found a remembrance in her Diary of the blue marks which in a fit of passion he had once inflicted on her arms. He saw that he had made her entirely miserable; that she had sacrificed her life to him; and that he had made a wretched return for her devotion. As soon as he could collect himself he put together a memoir of her, in which with deliberate courage he inserted the incriminating passages (by me omitted) of her Diary, the note of the blue marks among them, and he added an injunction of his own that, however stern and tragic that record might be, it was never to be destroyed.

It was now that I learnt to regard Carlyle with a more human feeling. My admiration of him had never wavered; but the contempt with which he treated everybody and everything, the anecdotes which I had heard from his wife, and his manifest forgetfulness of every other person's interest or comfort where his own wishes were concerned, had made it difficult for me to *like* him in the common sense of the word. He had seemed to me like a person apart from the rest of the world, with the mask of destiny upon him, to whom one could not feel exactly as towards a brother mortal. Another side of his character was now opened to me—the agony of his remorse for a long series of faults which now for the first time he saw in their true light. For the next four years I never walked with him without his recurring to a subject which was never absent from his mind. His conversation, however it opened, always drifted back into a pathetic cry of sorrow over things which were now irreparable. It was at once piteous and noble; for it was manifest that his faults, whatever they had been (and I did not then know completely what they had been), were no faults in his real nature. A repentance so deep and so passionate showed that the real nature was as beautiful as his intellect had been magnificent. He was still liable to his fits of temper. He was still scornful and overbearing and wilful; but it had become possible to love him—indeed, impossible not to love him.

It was in 1871, that suddenly, without a word of warning, without permission given or asked for, he one day brought to me a large parcel of papers. It contained a copy of the memoir which he had written of his wife, various other memoirs and fragments of biography, and a collection of his wife's letters to himself and other persons. He had put them together, he said, they were not completely prepared for publication, but he could do no more with them, nor could he tell what ought to be done with them. He gave them simply to me. Afterwards he seemed to have forgotten this, for he bequeathed them to me in his will. But at the time he said : 'Take these for my sake; they are yours to publish or not publish, as you please, after I am gone. Do what you will. Read them and let me know whether you will take them on these terms.' I did read them, and then for the first time I realised what a tragedy the life in Cheyne Row had been—a tragedy as stern and real as the story of Œdipus. The quarrels, I found to my sorrow, had been no surface differences of married life, but fierce and violent. Surely enough the remorse was needed. The collecting of those letters was an expiation, an expiation so frank and so complete that it washed the stain away. I for myself felt that he had done rightly, that his character never could be put fairly and honestly among the records of the great men to whom he belonged unless the faults were confessed and absolution granted on the only fitting terms. I felt at the time that he was laying upon me a cruel test of friendship, though he did not mean to be cruel. He ought to have come to a resolution himself, and not to have left the decision to me. I believed, however, that his hesitation rose from a sense that to order such a publication would seem ostentatious, as if his affairs were of so much consequence to mankind that he was entitled to call on them to occupy themselves with the seamy side of his life. At all events, and with the still uncompleted story in my hands, I told him my own opinion, that he had done right and that the letters ought to be brought out, but that if they were brought out, in justice both to her and to himself, his own memoir of his wife ought to be made known also. When he first wrote it he added a note forbidding its publication, but he had included it in the gift to me, and it had been copied out for that purpose. I might therefore have acted on his general instructions and dealt with it as I pleased, but I required and I received his own special permission, and on these terms the manuscripts remained with me.

I was so anxious, however, and I felt so seriously the load of the responsibility, that I asked him to allow me to consult John Forster, as it was too heavy for me to bear alone.

Forster read both memoir and letters. To me he gave no opinion. He said that he would speak to Carlyle about it, and I believe that he did. I do not know what passed between them. He said that he should tell Carlyle to make my position clear in his will, or trouble would come of it. This Carlyle did. He knew my own feeling, and never once to the end of his life, not once at any moment, did he give me a hint that he wished the letters suppressed. He left me always to the end under the impression that he wished them published, but he wished the act of publishing to be mine.

This incident, however, led to fuller communications between Forster and myself about Carlyle's history than we had ever exchanged before, and he told me a very singular story. I knew generally that the Carlyles had been very intimate with Lord Ashburton, then Mr. Baring, and his first wife, Lady Harriet Baring. I knew that the friendship had been more on Carlyle's side than on his wife's, who, I had gathered, generally, did not like Lady Harriet. But I had myself no acquaintance with the Ashburtons. I trouble myself as little as possible at all times with other people's affairs, and whether Mrs. Carlyle liked the people whom her husband liked was no matter to me. Forster, however, alluded to some mysterious secret in connection with the Ashburtons. When I said I knew nothing about it he seemed greatly surprised, and proceeded to tell me that Lady Ashburton had fallen deeply in love with Carlyle, that Carlyle had behaved nobly, and that Lord Ashburton had been greatly obliged to him. That Carlyle should behave nobly under such extraordinary circumstances seemed extremely likely to me, but I was greatly astonished. Lady Ashburton was a great lady of the world. Carlyle, with all his genius, had the manners to the last of an Annandale peasant. Wonderful things did happen—and women did strange things. I supposed that Forster must know what he was talking of. But if his account was true, I wondered why Mrs. Carlyle should seem so angry when Lady Ashburton's name was mentioned. She ought to have felt proud and amused. This too, however, was no business of mine, and I thought no more about it till two years later, when, just as before [in 1871, ed.] Carlyle had brought me the first parcel, he again [in 1873, ed.] sent me in a box a collection of letters, diaries, memoirs, miscellanies of endless sorts, the accumulations of a life. He told me that I must undertake his biography, and that there were the materials for me.

It happened that I had laid out my plans for the occupation of my later life in a way that would have been pleasant and profitable to me. I had finished my 'History of England.' I had nearly finished my 'English in Ireland.' After that my hands would be free. I foresaw, with the knowledge I already possessed, that I could not write a 'Life of Carlyle' that would have a chance of being popular. I foresaw that I should be involved in endless difficulties. To undertake it would involve the sacrifice of all the arrangements which I had made. It would be a certain loss in money. It would be fortunate for me if it did not lead me into perplexities which even at a distance looked sufficiently formidable. I had already, however, undertaken one dangerous part of the business. He seemed bent on my undertaking the rest. He had originally intended that no biography of himself should be written. He had said in his journal that there was a secret connected with him unknown to his closest friends, that no one knew and no one would know it, and that without a knowledge of it no true biography of him was possible. He never told me in words what this secret was, but I suppose he felt that I should learn it from his papers. At any rate, he had made up his mind that I was to do it, and I said that I would, provided I was left free to deal with the story exactly as I might think right, and that I was not to be interfered with. I set myself to study the enormous mass of manuscripts. I saw more than ever how complicated a task had been imposed on me, as the singular and tragical story unfolded itself. He had put these papers in my hands just as he had placed the others, with directions to burn freely as I might think right,—without an inventory, without a word to show that I was to render any further account of them.

I supposed them to have been given to me as the

memorials of his wife had been, and if he had any other intention he ought to have informed me of it. He did not. When any subject was disagreeable, it was his habit to thrust it away, and desire to hear no more of it. So these papers were thrust upon me, and so for seven years they remained. The picture which they presented was intensely interesting, in many respects intensely beautiful. His wife's journal, however, had come with the rest, and here was the explanation of part at least of the bitterness which had appeared in her letters. It was not, as Forster had told me, that Lady Ashburton had been ever devoted to Carlyle. That would have been no cause of complaint, and if Carlyle had behaved as Forster said, she would only have loved him the better for it. Quite evidently the feeling ran the other way. Carlyle had sate at the feet of the fine lady adoring and worshipping, had made himself the plaything of her caprices, had made Lady Ashburton the object of the same idolatrous homage which he had once paid to herself. What was the meaning of Forster's story? He died soon after, and I had no opportunity of asking him. But where had he learnt it? Of the actual truth there can be no doubt at all. It was no creation of Mrs. Carlyle's jealous fancies. There are in existence, or there were, masses of extravagant letters of Carlyle's to the great lady as ecstatic as Don Quixote's to Dulcinea. There was one even in which he had asked Lady Ashburton not to tell Mrs. Carlyle of some visit which he had paid to her, as she was so angry when she heard of his having been with her. It was of course the purest Gloriana worship, the homage of the slave to his imperious mistress. But such it was; while on the lady's side, whose letters after what Forster had said I looked into with interest, there was nothing else but the imperious mistress, to whom Carlyle was a passing amusement. It was not jealousy only on Mrs. Carlyle's part. She was ashamed and indignant at the unworthy position in which her husband was placing himself. Rinaldo in the bower of Armida or Hercules spinning silks for Omphale. What could Forster have been talking of? It seemed equally impossible (I think it was impossible) that Carlyle himself should have entertained any such extravagant notion. I did indeed know an instance of a peasant of high genius in whom another great lady took an admiring interest under somewhat analogous circumstances. A relation of the peasant who disliked the acquaintance persuaded him that the lady wanted to marry him. He was weak enough to believe it, and an intimacy which had lasted for many years was brought to an end. The vanity of the wisest will carry him far when he is flattered by a woman's attentions.

It is not conceivable to me that such a person

as Carlyle could ever have been so extravagantly deluded. At any rate, there was the story; a myth of a portentous kind already current. I tried once to approach the subject with Carlyle himself, but he shrank from it with such signs of distress that I could not speak to him about it again. He had put in my hands the letters and journals which told Mrs. Carlyle's view of it. He left them to speak for themselves.

This was one of the Cheyne Row secrets which was the cause of so much heart-burning and misery. But it was not all. Carlyle's mysterious allusion evidently did not refer to anything connected with Lady Ashburton. I am not sure that I know now what he meant; but a mystery was communicated to me, if I can call that a mystery, which had forced itself upon me from the study of the papers—something which I would infinitely rather have remained in ignorance of, because I could not forget it, because it must necessarily influence me in all that I might say, while I considered I must endeavour if possible to conceal it.

Geraldine Jewsbury was Mrs. Carlyle's most intimate and most confidential friend. Their correspondence, a large part of which Miss Jewsbury gave me, and which is now in my possession, proves sufficiently how close the confidence was. Geraldine herself was a gifted woman. She had been attracted by Carlyle's writings, had introduced herself to him as one of his most ardent worshippers, which to the end of her own life she continued to be in spite of all which she saw and knew. She was about Mrs. Carlyle's own age. She was admitted into Cheyne Row on the closest terms. Mrs. Carlyle, in her own troubles, spoke and wrote of Geraldine Jewsbury as her Consuelo. I had myself some external acquaintance with Miss Jewsbury. When she heard that Carlyle had selected me to write his biography she came to me to say that she had something to tell me which I ought to know. I must have learnt that the state of things had been most unsatisfactory; the explanation of the whole of it was that 'Carlyle was one of those persons who ought never to have married.' Mrs. Carlyle had at first endeavoured to make the best of the position in which she found herself. But his extraordinary temper was a consequence of his organisation. As he grew older and more famous, he had become more violent and overbearing. She had longed for children, and children were denied to her. This had been at the bottom of all the quarrels and all the unhappiness.

The nature of the relationship between the Carlyles I was not unprepared to hear. I had felt all along that there must be some mystery of the kind. Indeed, as I have already said, there were floating suspicions long before in the circle of Cheyne Row.

That Mrs. Carlyle had resented it was new to me. I had supposed that probably in the struggling and forlorn circumstances in which they began their married life they had agreed, being both of them singular persons, that they would do better without a family. Miss Jewsbury entirely dispelled this supposition. She said that Mrs. Carlyle never forgave the injury which she believed herself to have received. She had often resolved to leave Carlyle. He, of course, always admitted that she was at liberty to go if she pleased.

A fresh light was thus thrown on the Lady Ashburton affair. Intellectual and spiritual affection being all which he had to give, Mrs. Carlyle naturally looked on these at least as exclusively her own. She had once been his idol, she was now a household drudge, and the imaginative homage which had been once hers was given to another. This had been the occasion of the most violent outbreaks between them.

I had observed in Mrs. Carlyle's Diary that immediately after the entry of the blue marks on her arms, she had spent a day with Geraldine at Hampstead. I asked Miss Jewsbury if she recollected anything about it: she remembered it only too well. The marks were made by personal violence. Geraldine did not acquit her friend in all this. She admitted that she could be extremely provoking.

She said to me that Carlyle was the nobler of the two. Her veneration for her teacher never flagged in spite of all. She looked on his failings as aberrations due to his physical constitution. But the facts were as she told me. She did not live long after this. In her last illness, when she knew that she was dying, and when it is entirely inconceivable that she would have uttered any light or ill-considered gossip, she repeated all this to me, with many curious details. I will mention one, as it shows that Carlyle did not know when he married what his constitution was. The morning after his wedding-day he tore to pieces the flower-garden at Comeley Bank in a fit of ungovernable fury. The London life was a protracted tragedy. When the intimacy with the Ashburton house became established, she had definitely made up her mind to go away, and even to marry another person. She told him afterwards on how narrow a chance it had turned. His answer hurt her worse than any other word she ever heard from him: 'Well, I do not know that I should have missed you; I was very busy just then with Cromwell.'

She still admired him, even loved him in a sense for the beautiful and noble traits in his character. His letters to her when they were separated were uniformly tender and affectionate; so extreme indeed was the contrast between the letters and present realities that she used to say bitterly that he wrote them for his biographer. Still she knew that essentially he was generous, upright, and true. Having begun the sacrifice of herself, she struggled to carry it through for better or for worse as she had promised; the trial, however, was so protracted that when her health began to fail it seemed more than she could bear. She would not make a scandal by revealing the truth and dissolving her marriage, but once at least she had resolved to put herself out of the way altogether. She was to have gone to Scotland by sea. She meant in the darkness to have dropped over the stern and disappeared in such a way that it might seem as if her death had been an accident. Something prevented the sea voyage, but Geraldine's entire conviction was that, had she gone that way, she would never have been seen again. The life in Cheyne Row was to her, as Mrs. Carlyle said, like keeping a madhouse. Her entire system was shattered by the scenes which were continually recurring. She broke down at last with the strangest illness that ever woman died of.

I have since learnt that the nature of Carlyle's constitution was known to several persons, that in fact it was an open secret. Perhaps it was discovered by the physicians who attended in Mrs. Carlyle's illness. Perhaps she herself revealed her wrongs to more than Geraldine. Miss Jewsbury's information was given to me under too solemn circumstances, and was coupled with too many singular details, to allow doubt to be possible. It is as certain as anything human can be certain that what she related to me was what Mrs. Carlyle had related to her, and to all who knew Mrs. Carlyle that is evidence enough.

Any way, these things were communicated to me, and I was to be Carlyle's biographer. What was I to make of them? It was so weird, so uncanny a business that the more I thought of it the less could I tell what to do. I could well understand now how grave the occasion for Carlyle's remorse, which I had often thought morbid and exaggerated. I found myself entangled in painful family differences of exactly the kind which I most disliked to hear of, and acquaintance with which I had always avoided. It was all left to my discretion, but how was my discretion to be exercised? Carlyle's faults had been great, and he had endeavoured to make an atonement for them. It was an atonement complete in itself, so complete that he himself directed the publication of the memoir of his wife with her own letters; it swept the faults away and exhibited his real character in its brightest and tenderest light. If I suppressed all that—if I made my biography a mere panegyric on his writings and his generally noble and self-denying life, I should nevertheless give the world nothing but a mockery. Legends like that which I had heard from Forster were already flying. Innumerable letters were scattered about, from which partial and incorrect versions of his history would inevitably be passed into currency. I knew from anonymous letters, written to myself, that the state of things in Cheyne Row was no secret at all. The lives of great men are scrutinised to the bottom. Mankind will not rest, and do not rest till they have learnt all that can be discovered about such men. The lives of Swift, of Byron, and a hundred others were standing examples. Had I a right to keep concealed an authentic narrative compiled by Carlyle himself, in which he frankly acknowledged his own errors? I was not blind to the risk which I should run so far as I myself was personally concerned, but Carlyle was one of those rare and exceptional men who had exerted an immense influence on his own age. In my opinion, that influence would continue and would enlarge; and in such instances men are entitled to know everything which can be known of the character of those who have addressed them from the elevated position of prophet and teacher.

My acquaintance with the graver aspects of the story had, on the whole, not impaired my admiration of Carlyle. Taken for all in all, I admired him no

less. I loved him better for the feeling which he
had shown. He was human; he had his faults like
other men. The consequences had been miserable.
But he was miserable himself when he thought of
them. I felt as if I had never realised how great a
man he was till I saw what he suffered. I supposed
that what I felt myself would be felt by others, when
they had taken time to consider, but I did know that
the first impression would be a painful one. I could
not tell what it would be wise to do or what it
would be right to do. I continued to work at his
papers, to copy for myself the most important of his
manuscripts, since I could trust no other to do it for
me, and I put off my final decision till Carlyle himself
should be gone and I could think more calmly over
my responsibilities and of the manner in which I was
to act. I anticipated as not unlikely the resentment
of relations, but Carlyle had selected me apparently
because I was not a relation and would be free from
influences of a private kind.

The position became more complicated when,
about a year before his death, he suddenly said
one day to me when we were driving in a carriage,
'When you have done with those papers of mine
give them to Mary,' 'Mary' being his niece, Miss
Aitken,[1] who had lately married her cousin and was
living with Carlyle in Cheyne Row. Hitherto I had

[1] Mrs. Alexander Carlyle.

looked on those papers as my own. He had empowered me to burn freely. They had then been in my hands for six years, and he had never hinted to me that they were intended to pass out of my possession.

Of course I acquiesced, but for many reasons I felt uneasy. I had been trusted with the most delicate and difficult of responsibilities. My action, whatever it might be, would be open to objection of one sort or another, as no one knew better than Carlyle, since he could not decide for himself. If he had intended that these papers should be made use of by others, and in opposition to the judgment at which I should arrive should that judgment not coincide with theirs, then he was not dealing fairly with me. No one would undertake so dangerous a task on such conditions. He ought to have given me the opportunity of deciding whether under this arrangement I would go on with it; and could I have guessed that I should be treated as I have been treated, of course I should at once and with infinite relief have restored my trust into his hands. I was content, most incautiously, with a promise that Mary Carlyle would do nothing without consulting me and without my consent. Of course I should have gratefully acknowledged errors into which I might have fallen and misreading of his handwriting, which at the end of his life became almost illegible. I should have welcomed and encouraged any more satisfactory biography should my own seem insufficient or inaccurate. I was not prepared for, and I ought not to have encountered, a passionate and angry challenge of my right to make the revelations which were left to me to make or not to make. I was not prepared for attacks on my character as a gentleman and a man of honour. I acquit Carlyle of having meant this. He was incapable of treachery, least of all to me. But faith has not been kept with me. I see now—I saw it before, but I was unwilling to worry him—that I ought to have insisted on receiving from him in writing his own distinct directions. If they were not satisfactory to me I could then have declined to go on.

There were other reasons why Carlyle should not have been contented with a mere instruction that I was to give the papers to his niece, and why he should have given specific orders about them. I had believed them to be my property, and that he had given them to me. I believed, as being mine, I could give them to her, and that if this was not so questions would inevitably arise as to the legal ownership, and the consequent right to the profits of publication. He had made me one of his executors, though I did not know it. In his will he had left his papers to his brother John. This, too, I did not know, and I ought to have been informed of it; but his brother died before him, and the bequest lapsed, and then Mary Carlyle informed myself and my co-executor that the papers had been given to her by word of mouth, as I supposed them to have been given to me. She had no writing to give in evidence. If it was so, I had again been treated unfairly, for I ought to have been informed of it; but all was left uncertain, all was in confusion. The executors did not know, and do not know now, to whom the papers in law belonged. We agreed to act on Carlyle's verbal instruction to me, and to give them to Mary Carlyle, as he had said; but whether they were mine to give, or ours to give, is still an open question.

It was a question of no importance in itself, but it was important as affecting the right of property on publication. Not a word having been said upon the subject, and the whole undertaking having been thrust upon me, I assumed as a matter of course that the copyright and the profits of it would be mine whatever they might be, and that I might dispose of them as I thought fit. By this time I had drifted towards a cowardly conclusion that I would suppress Mrs. Carlyle's letters after all, that I would write a biography such as would most surely be to my own advantage, dwelling on all that was best and brightest in Carlyle, and passing lightly over the rest. I wrote the first volume of the 'Life' as it now stands in this sense. I had found among the papers the 'Reminiscences' of old Mr. James Carlyle, of Irving, of Jeffrey, of Wordsworth, and Southey. They were written, all but the account of his father, after Mrs. Carlyle's death. I thought them extremely beautiful. I thought they gave the most favourable picture of Carlyle himself which could possibly be conveyed. I thought that they ought to be published as they stood in a separate volume. I proposed it to him and he readily assented.[1]

So the matter rested till three months before Carlyle's death. Had nothing more happened I should have brought out the 'Reminiscences' in the form which I first proposed, have buried or burnt Mrs. Carlyle's letters and Carlyle's memoir of her, and finished my biography as I had begun, and the real story would, through me at least, never have been known. One day, however, on one of our drives (I was with him constantly, as I had been for many years, walking or driving), he began upon the 'Letters and Memorials,' and asked me what I had finally decided to do. He knew what my own feeling had originally been—that the intended collection of those 'Letters' was the most heroic act of his life; that they ought to be published, and the 'Memoir' published along with them. He had then been evidently pleased. He left it all to me. At my own desire he had allowed me to consult Forster; but

[1] The first of the two passages given in the Appendix occurs here.

Forster had given me no advice at all, and was now dead. I had not told Carlyle that my own mind had begun to waver about it, and I had never entered on the subject again, because I was afraid he would be disappointed, or would say something which would make it more difficult for me to do what I had brought myself to intend. He himself, however, began to speak about it exactly in the tone which I had feared: in the old melancholy, heart-broken way which I knew so well. I had not the courage to tell him that I had changed my mind. Indeed, I had not changed my mind so far as the right and wrong were concerned. I had been merely cowardly. I told him that the 'Letters' should be published and the 'Memoir' also. He seemed at once relieved and easy. He said I must do as I pleased. He never gave me any order. Then and always he avoided giving any order. He threw the responsibility on me; but neither then, nor at any time before, or after, from the first time in 1871, when he placed the manuscripts in my hands, did he ever indicate in the slightest degree that he himself had any reluctance or doubt about the propriety of the publication. If he ever spoke in a different tone to others, again I have been unfairly dealt with. To me the expression of such a doubt would have been more than welcome. To me, if to any one, that doubt ought to have been communicated.

This being so settled, I made up my mind to the worst. The whole story must now come out. I thought that still I might keep back the secrets which Geraldine Jewsbury had told me, but the main facts which appeared in the letters would now have to be brought out, except what I could not bring myself to print, the fatal passage in the Diary about the marks on the arm. Instead of it I would insert another extract from the same Diary which explained the cause of the quarrel, suppress such passages as would hurt other people, and thus once for all discharge myself of the whole burden. The 'Memoir of Mrs. Carlyle' I proposed to attach to the 'Reminiscences,' recomposed in part from the other notes and fragments which he had given to me. In view of what was to come and in order to show how true his affection had really been all along, in order to show what she had been—because when her letters appeared the blame of much might be thrown upon her—for both their sakes I was satisfied that the 'Memoir' had better appear at once, and those tender and suffering passages which I was universally reproached for having published, I thought and I still think, were precisely those which would win and command the pity and sympathy of mankind. The story, I often said to myself, was as sternly tragic, as profoundly pathetic as the great Theban drama. The genuine and heartfelt expression of remorse and sorrow must touch the very deepest chords of every serious heart.

Carlyle died, and the book came out. It was received with a violence of censure for which I was wholly unprepared. It was received also with an indignation of a different kind from Mary Carlyle and her friends. They were surprised and angry at the appearance of the 'Memoir,' being ignorant of what had passed about it between Carlyle and myself. They expected, I suppose, that the publication of the 'Memoir' would involve the publication of the 'Letters,' which I, as well as they, would have willingly avoided if I could.

Another and more paltry cause of disagreement had arisen simultaneously in a form at which I confess I was astonished. I had thought I was standing clear in the money part of the business; I had to find myself mistaken.

Here Mr. Froude refers at some length to certain complications which arose from the publication of the 'Reminiscences' in the United States, and from a claim preferred by Mrs. A. Carlyle to the literary profits of the book. These matters are only important from the consequences to which they led, and have therefore been omitted from the text in order that they might not interfere with the continuity of the narrative, but the original passages are given in their integrity at the end of Sir James Stephen's letter, in which the legal aspect of Mrs. A. Carlyle's claim is fully discussed. (*Appendix*, pp. 64–70.)

Though I had accepted Mary Carlyle's version of my engagement to give her the literary profits of the 'Reminiscences,' the copyright was still mine. I had restored the originals to her as Carlyle had directed; but I retained the literary control. More than once inquiries had been made of me through her lawyers when there would be any further money coming to her from other editions. The book went out of print, and I was at some loss what to do, for, being unable to do anything in England, Mary Carlyle had applied to Mr. Charles Norton to bring out an edition in America. I saw it announced, with an intimation that it was to appear at the desire of Carlyle's family, and that the edition which I had published was full of printer's blunders. I thought, and I still think, that Mr. Norton ought to have communicated with me. I should have raised no difficulty. I knew that there might be many errors of the press in the book. Mary Carlyle has reminded me that I said her uncle's handwriting was beautiful. It was beautiful when he was in his vigour; after his hand began to shake it became harder to decipher than the worst manuscript which I have ever examined. I copied out the greater part of the 'Reminiscences' myself. A large part of them I copied twice; I had to work at them with a magnifying glass, and in many hundred instances I was at a loss to know exactly what particular words might be. My own hand is not a good one, and there was a further source of error in the printer's reading of this. At least I was not careless, except perhaps that I had found the manuscript so difficult that in reading the proofs I trusted too much to my own transcript. The 'Memoir' of Mrs. Carlyle was printed directly from the copy which Carlyle gave me. If there were mistakes in this the fault did not rest with me. I was not surprised, however, when I heard that the book required much correction. I do not let judgment go by default. When I was so often in doubt myself, others may have been wrong and I may have been right, but I did not and I do not stand upon this. I waited for the promised American edition to make the necessary corrections. For some reason it did not appear. A new edition was called for. I thought that the right of editing ought to lie with the possessor of the originals. I therefore frankly surrendered my own right unconditionally, and the result is the edition now published. I should have raised no objection if Mr. Norton had himself applied to me. It would have been more courteous had he done so. For the rest, I went on with my task and I finished in the best way that I could, amidst threatened lawsuits, lawyers' letters pressing for the papers, feeling throughout that I was handling burning coals and under a hailstorm of unfavourable criticism, which under the circumstances was perfectly natural. I was keeping back the essential part of the story which had governed my own action, and the world, not knowing the full truth, considered that I made too much of trifles which need not have been spoken of at all. If I have now told all, it is because I see that nothing short of it will secure me the fair judgment to which I am entitled. I am certain that I have done the best for Carlyle's own memory. The whole facts are now made known. The worst has been said that can be said, and anything further which can now be told about him can only be to his honour; already the tendency is to acquit Carlyle and lay the blame (such blame as there is) upon her. The usual custom is to begin with the brightest side and to leave the faults to be discovered afterwards. It is dishonest and it does not answer. Of all literary sins Carlyle himself detested most a false biography. Faults frankly acknowledged are frankly forgiven. Faults concealed work always like poison. Burns's offences were made no secret of. They are now forgotten, and Burns stands without a shadow on him the idol of his countrymen. Byron's 'Diary' was destroyed, and he remains and will remain with a stain of suspicion about him which revives and will revive, and will never be wholly obliterated. 'The truth shall make you free' in biography as in everything. Falsehood and concealment are a great man's worst enemies.

Such at least is the doctrine about the matter which I learnt from Carlyle himself; such is my own opinion, and on this I have acted. I cannot discover in myself any other motive for the course which I have taken. All motives of worldly prudence lay the other way. Personally I never met with anything but the warmest kindness from Carlyle. I had no secret injuries to resent. I had always admired him, and in his later days I learnt to love him. No one does what he knows to be wrong without some object. If any one will suggest what unworthy motive I can have had, he may perhaps assist me in discovering it. I cannot discover it myself.

It is likely enough that I have made mistakes in matters of fact as well as in the reading of the manuscripts. Let all such be made known. No one will be better pleased than I shall be. I complain only of reflections on my good faith and personal honesty, which I fling off me with legitimate indignation.

I am told that Mary Carlyle possesses documents which show parts of Carlyle's story in another light. If so, they ought to have been communicated to me. She says now that they were considered too sacred. I cannot help that. I could judge only by what

Carlyle put into my hands. She offered to show them to my solicitor. If too sacred for me to see, they were too sacred to be exposed to a lawyer. If she wished me to know what they contained she ought to have sent me copies, or have told me generally their contents.

It is of no importance now. The manuscripts and all that is in them are in her hands. She has released herself from the engagements which were made with me. I am quit of it and for ever. I have made many blunders—the worst and greatest that when I knew what the circumstances were I did not at once decline to have anything to do with them. I was misled by a too confiding admiration of Carlyle's own heroism. It was unwise of me, and I regret my imprudence too late.

When Carlyle decided that his niece was to have the manuscripts after I had done with them, I ought not to have been contented with a promise. I ought to have insisted on his defining precisely and with his own hand the respective positions in which we were to stand. He was impatient of being spoken to on a subject which he wished to thrust from him. I concluded that he would himself have left in writing something that was to guide me. He left nothing.

If I have erred in other ways I may plead the worry and perplexity in which I was involved and the nature of my task, which perhaps the wisest man could not have dealt with without stumbling in places. My book, if it is still to be condemned at present, will be of use hereafter. A hundred years hence, the world will better appreciate Carlyle's magnitude. The sense of his importance, in my opinion, will increase with each generation. The unwillingness to look closely into his character will be exchanged for an earnest desire to know all which can be ascertained about him, and what I have written will then have value. It may not be completely correct, but it will have made concealment impossible, and have ensured that the truth shall be known. The biographies of the great men of the past, the great spiritual teachers especially, with whom Carlyle must be ranked, are generally useless. They are idle and incredible panegyrics, with features drawn without shadows, false, conventional, and worthless. The only 'Life' of a man which is not worse than useless is a 'Life' which tells all the truth so far as the biographer knows it. He may be mistaken, but he has at least been faithful, and his mistakes may be corrected. So perhaps may some of mine, especially if particular papers have been purposely withheld from me.

I have discharged the duty which was laid on me as faithfully as I could. I have nothing more to reveal, and, as far as I know, I have related exactly everything which bears on my relations with Carlyle and his history. This is all that I can do, and I have written this that those who care for me may have something to rely upon if my honour and good faith are assailed after I am gone.

    Written in Cuba, Vedado,
        March 12–15, 1887.

LETTER FROM SIR JAMES STEPHEN TO MR. FROUDE.[1]

THE LATE MR. CARLYLE'S PAPERS.

HAVING been exposed to much criticism for my conduct about Mr. Carlyle's papers, and being reluctant to enter into any public controversy on the subject, I asked my friend Sir James Stephen, who himself managed a great part of the matter, to give me his account of it. I have had my letter to him, and his answer, printed. So far as he relates anything the knowledge of which he derived from me, he has related accurately what I told him. The remainder rests on his own authority and on that of the documents, the bearing of which he understands better than I can do.

The points in discussion do not touch the larger issue whether I have done well or ill in the discharge of my duty as Carlyle's biographer, but it is better that these points should be cleared up than that they should remain to confuse the broader question.

ONSLOW GARDENS: *December* 9, 1886.

J. A. FROUDE.

5 ONSLOW GARDENS: *November* 30, 1886.

MY DEAR STEPHEN,—The question of my action in connexion with Carlyle's biography having been again raised with some acrimony, I venture to ask you to put in writ-

[1] The following pages were printed in pamphlet form in 1886 for private circulation.

ing your own impressions on a part of the matter with which you, as my fellow-executor, were immediately concerned. I am unwilling, for many reasons, to prolong a personal controversy, as if I thought that my own conduct required defence: but life is uncertain; it will be more satisfactory to me to know that there is an authoritative statement in existence, to which, if circumstances make it necessary, an appeal may hereafter be made. I am not now speaking of the larger contention, whether I made a right use of the discretionary powers which were entrusted to me as to the publication of Mr. Carlyle's letters. A subsidiary question was raised, as you know, on the ownership of the materials which I used for the 'Reminiscences' and for the 'Biography.' Claims were put forward, as a matter of right, on the profits arising from the former of these publications; and where I had supposed myself to be acting liberally (I might almost say with generosity) of my own free will, I was met with threats of a legal action. You are aware of everything that took place. You are in a position which no one else occupies, or can occupy, to relate all the circumstances completely and impartially. I am not asking for a report which can be published, but for a narrative and a judgment, to which I, or my friends after me, may be able to refer should a continuance of the controversy seem to make such a reference desirable. I hope that you will consider my request a reasonable one, and will not refuse to comply with it. Yours faithfully,

J. A. FROUDE.

32 DE VERE GARDENS: *December* 9, 1886.

MY DEAR FROUDE,—At your request I put into writing what I know of your connexion with the papers of Mr. Carlyle which formed the materials of your works about him and his wife. The story is long and intricate, but the facts can for the most part be ascertained beyond dispute, as most of them are stated in three voluminous correspondences—one between Messrs. Farrer, the solicitors to Mr. Carlyle's executors, and myself, on one side, and Messrs. Benson, Mrs. Alexander Carlyle's solicitors, on the other; the other two between your solicitor (Mr. Leman) and Mrs. Alexander Carlyle's solicitors (Messrs. Benson). All these and many other papers I have carefully examined before writing this letter. Parts of it rest on what you at various times have told me. Some of the papers are in the possession of Messrs. Benson, and these I have not seen since they were written.

The story is this.

Mrs. Carlyle died in April 1866. Mr. Carlyle, after her death, passed much of his time in writing and arranging papers relating to her. In particular he wrote in a memorandum book an account of her which formed the principal material for the sketch of her life published in the second volume of the 'Reminiscences.' To this he added a note, saying in solemn terms that it was not in case of his death to be published as it stood. This you tell me was written in 1866, or soon afterwards. I call it the Sketch.

After this Mr. Carlyle put together a number of letters and other matters, which he called a 'Memorial of Jane Welsh Carlyle.' Mrs. Alexander Carlyle made by his directions a fair copy of both the Memorial and the Sketch. This fair copy was placed in your hands in 1871. The original letters and draft remained with her, with the exception of the original Sketch just mentioned, which was delivered to you.

On February 6, 1873, Mr. Carlyle made his will. He left the Memorial to you absolutely, 'with whatever other fartherances and elucidations may be possible,' which words you regarded as covering the Sketch. He added elaborate provisions as to your consulting his brother, Dr. Carlyle, and Mr. Forster as to the publication of these matters. The three, he said, 'will make earnest survey of the MS. and its subsidiaries there or elsewhere.' He adds 'The manuscript is by no means ready for publication; nay, the questions, How, when (after what delay—seven, ten years) it or any portion of it should be published are still dark to me, but on all such points James Anthony Froude's practical summing-up and decision is to be taken as mine.'

The direction as to Dr. Carlyle and Mr. Forster became inoperative by the fact of their dying in Mr. Carlyle's lifetime, and in your view both the Memorial and the Sketch became under these provisions yours absolutely, with an express direction to use your discretion as to publication, overruling the note appended to the Sketch.

The 'imperfect copy' and the original letters which Mrs. Alexander Carlyle had copied were bequeathed to her. The rest of his MSS. Mr. Carlyle bequeathed to his brother Dr. Carlyle, directing that one of them, a sketch of his father, should be 'preserved in the family.' On Dr. Carlyle's death this bequest lapsed, and the documents not specially bequeathed in the will or otherwise disposed of during his lifetime passed to the executors of the will by the general bequest of all personal property.

Dr. Carlyle, you, and I were made executors by a codicil dated November 8, 1878, and Dr. Carlyle having died in his brother's lifetime, you and I took out probate.

So far as the will was concerned no difficulty arose, at least no legal difficulty, but after the making of his will Mr. Carlyle dealt with his papers in a way which caused much embarrassment. The will says, 'Express biography of me I had really rather that there should be none.'

Upon this point Mr. Carlyle changed his mind, and not very long after the will, either in the course of the year 1873, or at all events not later than the beginning of 1874, he sent to you as materials for his biography a great mass of papers and MS. books without any sort of inventory or written directions of any sort. Verbally, he told you to do as you pleased with them, adding in particular that you were to 'burn freely.' The sketch of his father and the other papers used as materials for the 'Reminiscences' were amongst these, or were sent afterwards.

Mrs. Alexander Carlyle informed us through her solicitors, some months after her uncle's death, that in 1875 he made a verbal gift to her of all his papers, and gave her his keys. Of this gift neither you nor I had any notice till we were informed of it by Mrs. Alexander Carlyle's solicitors in June 1881.

About a year before his death Mr. Carlyle told you that after you had done with the papers to be used for his biography you were to give them back to Mrs. Alexander Carlyle.

All this afterwards gave rise to three distinct views as to the property in the papers not disposed of by the will. You considered that they were yours by a gift accompanied by delivery, but you admitted yourself to be bound, morally at least, to give them to Mrs. Alexander Carlyle after you had written the biography. Mrs. Carlyle claimed them as hers in virtue of the gift which, as she said, was made to her in 1875. Lastly, the executors were advised that, notwithstanding the delivery of the papers to you, those which were not specifically bequeathed passed to the executors under the general bequest of personal estate. The effect of this upon the right of the residuary legatees to the proceeds and copyright of the works was a separate question of much delicacy.

There was a further distinct question, or set of questions, about the 'Reminiscences.' Your account to me of what took place is that not long before Mr. Carlyle's death it occurred to you that it would be well to publish in a separate form his accounts of his father, of Irving, and of Lord Jeffrey. Your first plan was that he should edit them, but this he was unable to do; you also meant to publish in America, being led to believe that a very large profit would be made there, and you promised to give the whole profits of the American edition to Mrs. A. Carlyle, but owing to circumstances these profits became very small. You then formed an intention, which you believe you afterwards expressed in a letter to her, to give her half the profits of your 'Biography' as well as the 'Reminiscences;' but her view on the other hand appeared to be that she was entitled to the whole of the profits of the 'Reminiscences,' wherever published, by your promise, and further that she was entitled by Mr. Carlyle's gift to the whole of the papers necessary for writing his life, but this last claim was never known either to you or to me till June 1881.

Apart from this, before publication and after your promise, whatever it was, you altered the plan of the 'Reminiscences' and included in it the sketch of the life of Mrs. Carlyle, entitled 'Jane Welsh Carlyle,' which formed a third of the whole work.

Mr. Carlyle died on February 4, 1881. On February 21, 1881, I called on Mrs. Alexander Carlyle and had a long conversation with her, of which I there and then made a memorandum, which is now before me. I showed it to her and her husband, and I sent her a copy of it next day. I never received from her any disclaimer of its correctness. Mr. Ouvry (Mr. Farrer's late partner), who was then acting as solicitor for all parties, and Mr. Alexander Carlyle were present on the occasion. At the time when the memorandum was made I was very superficially acquainted with these matters. The memorandum is as follows:

Memorandum of Mrs. A. Carlyle's understanding of the facts relating to Mr. Carlyle's papers.

1. Papers relating to the late Mr. Carlyle bequeathed to Mr. Froude by the will of Mr. Carlyle. These papers Mrs. A. Carlyle considers to be Mr. Froude's absolutely.

2. The papers relating to Mr. Carlyle's father, Mr. Irving, and Lord Jeffrey, intended to be published under the title of 'Reminiscences,' Mrs. A. Carlyle also understands to have been given to Mr. Froude after the death of Mr. Forster, though she does not know what may have passed between Mr. Carlyle and Mr. Froude on the subject. She, however, says that Mr. Froude some time ago promised to give to her the whole of the proceeds of the 'Reminiscences' when published, and that she informed her uncle of this intention, and that he approved of it, and under these circumstances she declines to receive any share of the proceeds less than the whole.

3. The papers relating to Mr. Carlyle and intended to serve as materials for his biography. These papers Mrs. A. Carlyle understands to have been given to Mr. Froude, so that the property in them passed to him. She also understands that her uncle intended that any profit to be derived from the book, for which they are to be materials, was to go to Mr. Froude, and she has no wish to interfere in any way with Mr. Froude's discretion as to the use to be made of these papers; on the other hand, Mrs. A. Carlyle considers that Mr. Froude ought not to burn or otherwise destroy any of these papers, but to return them to

her (Mrs. A. Carlyle) after the biography for which they are to be used as materials is published.

J. F. STEPHEN.

February 21, 1881.

This was written in the presence of Mr. and Mrs. Carlyle and Mr. Ouvry, and was accepted by Mrs. Carlyle as a full statement of her views. I sent her a copy of it this day, February 22, 1881.—J. F. S.

This memorandum gives no hint of the gift of papers afterwards alleged to have been made to Mrs. A. Carlyle in 1875. It states as to the 'Reminiscences,' that, as you had promised her the whole of the proceeds of the 'Reminiscences,' she would not take less. I was not at that time aware that you had made any proposal to her about the profits of any other work about Mr. Carlyle, nor did I know the precise details of what you have since told me till very lately. I had told her that you proposed to give her half, and you afterwards told me that the original promise was to give her the whole profits of an edition not comprising the Sketch, to be published in America, and that your offer of half of the proceeds of the English edition including the Sketch was regarded by you as equivalent to the falling short on the American edition excluding the Sketch. The probable proceeds of the American edition had, you told me, been originally represented to you as likely to be much greater than you found they would actually be. However this may be, it is obvious that Mrs. A. Carlyle at the time of the memorandum thought that your promise, whatever it was, had reference to an edition exclusive of the Sketch, as the memorandum enumerates all the papers contained in the 'Reminiscences' except the Sketch and the appendix entitled 'Reminiscences of Southey.'

With regard to the materials for the biography the memorandum says: 'These papers Mrs. Carlyle understands to have been given to Mr. Froude, so that the property passed to him.' I have a distinct independent recollection of the words which are here recorded. She was making a very diffuse statement as to the details, when I said, 'At all events they were given to Mr. Froude, so that the property passed to him.' She said, 'Yes.' The wording therefore was mine and not hers, though she accepted and never disclaimed it. No dispute had arisen at this time, nor did I expect any, but I thought her statement important and took it down.

The 'Reminiscences' were published soon afterwards. The MS. notebook containing the Sketch was on May 3 returned to Mrs. A. Carlyle (see her letter to Mr. Ouvry dated May 11). It was regarded as a part of the 'imperfect copy and original letters' bequeathed to her by Mr. Carlyle. Mrs. Alexander Carlyle was apparently much offended at the publication in the 'Reminiscences' of the Sketch, and a controversy between you and her in the 'Times' newspaper followed. She accused you (May 5, 1881) of violating Mr. Carlyle's express directions in publishing the Sketch. You replied (May 6) that the direction written in 1866 was revoked by the will made in 1873, which gave you absolute discretion as to publication, and you added that Mr. Carlyle was in his lifetime made aware of your intention to publish these papers. You have often told me in conversation how this was: that his mind was much exercised on the question whether the publication should take place or not; that he appeared to you to wish that it should, but that he wished the decision to be yours and not his; that you, thinking the publication proper, and wishing also to set his mind at rest, told him you meant to publish; that he said 'Very well,' seemed relieved and satisfied, and never afterwards returned to the subject. Substantially the same statement is made in the last volume of his biography, pp. 466–7.

Mrs. Alexander Carlyle wrote (May 7) to suggest that you should ' surrender the papers now to be examined and decided upon by three friends of Mr. Carlyle.' You (May 9) refused this suggestion, and said, ' The remaining letters (i.e. the materials for the biography), which I was directed to return to Mrs. Carlyle so soon as I had done with them, I will restore at once to any responsible person whom she will empower to receive them from me. I have reason to complain of the position in which I have been placed with respect to these MSS. They were sent to me at intervals without inventory or even a memorial list. I was told that the more I burnt of them the better, and they were for several years in my possession before I was aware that they were not my own. Happily I have destroyed none of them, and Mrs. Carlyle may have them all when she pleases.' You afterwards considered yourself entitled, and I entirely agreed with you, to refuse to carry out the intention thus expressed. It had no legal validity. It was a mere statement of your intention, and was at the most a voluntary promise, founded on no consideration, made in a moment of irritation, and which did not in any degree alter Mrs. Alexander Carlyle's position. If a man made an unqualified promise to leave all his property to another, he would, I think, be entitled to withdraw it at any time before it had affected the plans in life of the person to whom it was made.

To have given up the papers would have been to waste the labour of seven or eight years of your life, and to fail in carrying out the wish of Mr. Carlyle, that you should write his life, and your promise to him to do so.

Quite apart from this a further question arose. You

discovered soon after writing the letter of May 9 that you had no right to give the papers up without my consent. We were advised by counsel, on May 13, 1881, and upon a case which embodied your statement of the facts, that the papers in question belonged not to you personally but to Mr. Carlyle's executors, and that Mr. Carlyle's direction to give them up to Mrs. Alexander Carlyle when you had done with them was 'an attempted verbal testamentary disposition, which has no legal authority.' You could not therefore have given them up without my consent, and I never gave, or would have given, it.

I saw Mrs. Alexander Carlyle, and heard from her several times upon this matter. I have only a general recollection of these interviews, which took place nearly six years ago. Mrs. A. Carlyle appears to have written me a letter of some importance, February 26 or 27, 1881, but I have not got it and do not remember its contents. On May 29, 1881, however, she wrote me a letter, in which she says, 'I should like very much to accept your offer to talk the matter over with my solicitor, but, strictly speaking, I have at present no solicitor of my own entirely acquainted with the case. Messrs. —— act for me ; but, as it appeared to friends of mine who have taken a very kind interest in the case that they had nothing practical to suggest, these friends, with my permission, have stated the facts to their solicitor, who is drawing up a case for an opinion of counsel. I have given them copies of the most important papers in my possession relating to the subject, and have told them all the facts I know, some of which have only lately come to my knowledge, and of the importance of most of which I was not myself aware.' It is obvious from this that, till she talked over the matter with the friends referred to, she was not aware of the importance of her conversation with Mr. Carlyle in 1875.

On May 31 I received a letter from Mr. Benson, the gentleman referred to as the solicitor of Mrs. Alexander Carlyle's friends. It states that he is drawing up a case, and the case itself must, from further letters, have been sent to me early in June, though I cannot give the exact date. The case was returned to Mrs. Alexander Carlyle's solicitor, and I have no copy of it, but I well recollect its principal statement, and my recollection is confirmed by references to it in subsequent letters in the hands of Mr. Farrer. The effect of it was that in the year 1875 Mr. Carlyle had made a present verbally of all his papers to Mrs. Alexander Carlyle, and had given her the keys of the receptacles which contained them. I had never heard a hint of this before; it appeared to me to be extremely difficult to reconcile with the delivery of the MSS. to you, though I did not then know at what precise time it had taken place, and it seemed inconsistent with the statement which she made to me, as recorded in my memorandum of February 21. You were afterwards able to state positively that the papers said to have been given by Mr. Carlyle to Mrs. Alexander Carlyle, in 1875, were delivered to you not later than the very beginning of 1874, and probably in 1873. Your reason was that you remembered observations made by your late wife, who died in February 1874, on matters of personal interest to her contained in the papers. Of course, if the documents were put into your possession in 1873, with directions to burn what you pleased, it was difficult to believe that in 1875 they were comprehended in a verbal gift made to Mrs. Alexander Carlyle, of which gift no notice was given to you. If in 1873 they were, as Mrs. Alexander Carlyle told me in February 1881, given to you 'so as to pass the property in them,' they were not Mr. Carlyle's to give in 1875. Besides, it is a rule of law that a claim upon a dead man's estate cannot be admitted upon the uncorroborated statement of the claimant, and it appeared to me that there was no corroboration here. Several circumstances were mentioned in the case which, as Mrs. Alexander Carlyle's advisers contended, supplied the necessary corroboration, but I could not accept them as such. On June 10, 1881, I wrote to her solicitor, Mr. Benson, saying that I could not 'consent to the recognition of Mrs. Alexander Carlyle's claim as against the residuary legatees, unless and until it was duly established in a court of law,' and that you, as my co-executor, put yourself in my hands.

I expressed at the same time the opinion that, as between her and you, the matter might be easily settled. In order to explain what I proposed, I must go back a little. Whatever might have been the exact understanding between Mrs. Alexander Carlyle and yourself as to the proceeds of the 'Reminiscences,' you had long been prepared to let her have the whole of them except 300*l.*, which was to be reserved on account of your having edited the book, and of the fact that it included the sketch of Jane Welsh Carlyle, which was your property by the will. These profits amounted at that time, 'after the deduction of 300*l.*,' to 1,500*l.* and upwards, and subsequently reached 1,630*l.* You had paid about 1,500*l.* to Mr. Ouvry in May— namely, 1,400*l.* from the English edition and 100*l.* from an American edition. He had put it on deposit at Coutts's Bank in May (see his letter of May 13, 1881, to Mrs. A. Carlyle), but about that time I raised the question of the rights of the executors on behalf of the residuary legatees, and it remained at the bank at interest.

Again, it was clear that, whoever might be the actual proprietor of the papers used as materials for the biography, it was Mr. Carlyle's intention that you should use them until the biography was written, and that when it was

written you should return them to Mrs. Alexander Carlyle.
I therefore proposed that a deed should be drawn, to which
the residuary legatees were to be parties, reciting all these
facts and settling all questions by declaring that Mrs. A.
Carlyle should have all the past and future profits of the
'Reminiscences' except 300*l.*, you retaining the literary
control over the work; that you should keep the materials
of the biography till you had done with them, and that you
should then return them to Mrs. Alexander Carlyle, and
that the residuary legatees and executors should consent.

Much discussion followed. In the course of it the
residuary legatees consented to our settling the matter as
we thought fit, but Mrs. A. Carlyle refused to consent, on
the ground that the compromise gave her nothing but
what she was entitled to apart from your letter to the
'Times' of May 9, and apart from the alleged gift to her,
said to have been made in 1875, and that it practically
recognised your right to withdraw your letter of May 9,
already referred to. Her counter-offer was that you
should give up the papers and not complete your book, and
that you should, on the other hand, take the 1,500*l.* profits
on the 'Reminiscences.' We wholly refused this offer.
She afterwards proposed that the papers should be returned
to her, but that you should have access to them at her
house, and this also was refused. This discussion lasted
till the autumn of 1881.

At last, after many letters and several interviews,
Mr. Farrer wrote to Mr. Benson on October 15, 1881, the
following letter:

66 LINCOLN'S INN FIELDS, LONDON, W.C.:
October 15, 1881.

Carlyle's Executors.

DEAR SIR,—The executors have written to me to say that
they have fully considered the matter, and are not disposed to

modify the views which Sir James Stephen expressed to Mr. Benson at our office, that further discussion seems likely to lead to no good result, and that the offer then made must be accepted before November 1 or refused; and unless it is accepted as made, it will be considered as wholly withdrawn on that day. In that event Mr. Froude will withdraw every promise of every description he has made to Mrs. Carlyle, and will leave her to enforce any legal rights she may have. That there may be no misconception, I repeat the terms proposed by the executors.

1. Mr. Froude offers to make over to Mrs. Carlyle all the proceeds of the 'Reminiscences,' past or future, subject to a deduction of 300l. Mr. Froude is to retain the literary control over the book. Mrs. Carlyle's right to these proceeds is to be considered as arising solely from this agreement.

2. Mrs. Carlyle agrees that Mr. Froude shall keep the papers now in his possession as materials for the life of Mr. Carlyle until that work is completed, and that he shall use them as materials for that work. She also renounces all claim upon the copyright.

Mr. Froude agrees that the papers shall be given to Mrs. Carlyle when the work is completed or on his death.

It is understood on both sides that this does not apply to the Letters and Memorials of Jane Welsh Carlyle given by Mr. Carlyle to Mr. Froude in 1870 or 1871, and bequeathed to him by Mr. Carlyle's will.

3. If Mr. Froude and Mrs. Carlyle come to this agreement the executors will not press their claim either to the MSS. or to the proceeds of the 'Reminiscences.'

I may add that the Letters and Memorials of J. W. Carlyle bequeathed to Mr. F. by Mr. Carlyle's will were given to him in 1870 or 1871 by Mr. Carlyle, and consist of a large number of letters, all numbered, annotated, and with autobiographical matter prefixed and interspersed. Mr. Froude considers that these are his absolute property. With reference to the papers given to him in 1875 [1873], he considers not only that they are his property by Mr. Carlyle's gift, but that under the will he has a right to such of them as are illustrative of the Letters and Memorials of J. W. C.

Yours truly,
(Signed) FREDK. WILLIS FARRER.

I quote this letter at length because it expresses the position which we took up, and from which neither of us receded. It was followed by a long correspondence which lasted till August 3, 1882, and in which a great variety of matters were discussed. There was at first a prospect of an administration suit, and no express comprehensive settlement was ever made. Long letters were written, and proposals and counter-proposals were made. Our principal difficulty was to arrange for the payment of the 1,500*l.* without admitting Mrs. A. Carlyle's claim to the papers on which she founded her claim to the money. There was also a great deal of discussion as to the length of time during which you were to keep the papers, the steps by which they were to be delivered over to Mrs. A. Carlyle, and the making of an inventory of them. These matters were settled by degrees, and I think I may say on the terms which were stated in Mr. Farrer's letter of October 15, 1881. The stipulation that Mrs. Carlyle should admit that her right to the proceeds should be considered as arising from the agreement only, was, however, not insisted on.

On June 29, 1882, Mr. Benson, Mrs. A. Carlyle's solicitor, signed a receipt for four bundles of letters connected with the first part of the Biography of Carlyle, which was published in 1882. You had then done with these papers.

On August 3, 1882, Mr. Benson gave a receipt for Messrs. Farrer's cheque for the sum of 1,544*l.* 3*s.* 8*d.*, being the then proceeds of the 'Reminiscences,' less 300*l.* Mrs. A. Carlyle's receipt I have not seen, but I believe she gave one. No doubt she duly received the money. You afterwards paid her two sums of 120*l.* and 10*l.*, which you received from America, I think in 1882 and 1883.

There was never, so far as I know, any acknowledgment, written or otherwise, as to the terms on which the money was given or received. You always considered that from first to last the whole was voluntary generosity on your part. This also was and is my own opinion. She persistently claimed it as a right. This is, no doubt, the explanation of an apparent contradiction between Mrs. A. Carlyle and yourself in letters relating to Mr. Norton's publication about Mr. Carlyle. You said you had given her the proceeds of the 'Reminiscences.' She said (November 4, 1886), 'The assertion that I received the proceeds of the "Reminiscences" as a gift from Mr. Froude I simply deny, and can, if necessary, produce my lawyer's statement on the point.' Mrs. Carlyle has a right to her own opinion. Mine is that you paid the money voluntarily, and she received it as a right. She never sued for it, and I do not believe she could have recovered it if she had; for she could have claimed it as her own only on the ground that the MSS. were hers by virtue of a gift of Mr. Carlyle, a claim which I think no court would have acted upon on her uncorroborated assertion, especially if it were proved, as it could have been, that the papers were deposited with you more than a year before, as she said, they were given to her. It was my whole object throughout to prevent a lawsuit for the determination of what I felt was a merely speculative question, and to defeat the attempt made to prevent you from writing Mr. Carlyle's life, and I am happy to say I succeeded.

You finished the biography and published the two remaining volumes in 1884.

A long correspondence took place between your solicitor, Mr. Leman, and Mrs. A. Carlyle's solicitor, Mr. Benson, as to the delivery to her of the papers. There were various delays, owing to your absence abroad,[1] to your wish to make some final corrections, &c., but on December 5, 1884, your

[1] Mr. Froude went that summer to Norway.

solicitor handed the papers in two boxes to Mrs. Carlyle and took her receipt for them.

On March 28, 1885, Mr. Benson told Mr. Leman that she was 'much pleased at the contents of the boxes,' and Mr. Leman adds in his letter to you : ' It appears that they contained more papers than she had expected to find in them.' There was subsequent correspondence about a particular MS. which had been accidentally mislaid.

In 1885 a further correspondence took place about the assignment to Mrs. Carlyle of the copyright of the 'Reminiscences.' It ended by your assigning the copyright to her last June, protesting at the same time that you were under no contract to do so.

I have told the story at full length in order to put upon record the particulars of your conduct in all this matter. You appear to me to have acted throughout quite straightforwardly. You carried out precisely what from the first you acknowledged to be your moral obligations. Indeed, where only your own interests were concerned, you went beyond them ; for you accepted Mrs. A. Carlyle's recollection of the arrangement about the profits of the 'Reminiscences' instead of your own, and you gave up the claim to retain the literary control of that work—which you admittedly possessed—for the sake of peace. On the other hand, where your duty to Mr. Carlyle was in question you stood firm, and performed your promise to write his life and to use the materials which he had provided for that purpose, notwithstanding Mrs. A. Carlyle's attempts to prevent you from doing so, and in opposition to claims which she did not attempt to enforce by law. You returned the papers to Mrs. A. Carlyle when you had done with them, according to her uncle's wish, though you were advised that it was not legally binding. You gave Mrs. A. Carlyle above 1,600$l.$, which she could not have compelled you to give her, as your original promise was made voluntarily. No doubt she had a moral claim to a part of it, but to a large part of it she had no moral claim, except upon the supposition, which you accepted, that her recollection of conversations which took place about two years before was right and your own wrong. You were provoked into writing a hasty letter to the 'Times,' which you afterwards withdrew. It was a letter which imposed no legal obligation, and, as I think, no moral obligation, and you could not have fulfilled the intention which you there expressed without wasting the labour of eight years of your life, breaking a pledge to Mr. Carlyle to write his life, and violating a legal duty of which, when you wrote the letter, you were not aware. In a word, in your whole conduct I see nothing to regret, and I wish to add that I was just as much responsible for it morally as you were, though your letters were written independently of me.

Of Mrs. Alexander Carlyle I will say only that she took a view of the publication of the 'Reminiscences' which many people do take, and tried to stop the publication of the biography on what she believed to be valid legal grounds. I think she was erroneously advised; but the question is one of mere curiosity, which can never now be decided in an authoritative way.

I know you have suffered much worry and annoyance from all this matter, and this is the main reason why I have gone over it so fully. After a close intimacy of nearly thirty years, it would be impossible to me to believe that your conduct had fallen short of the highest standard of truth and honour. The whole difficulty in this matter arose from the feebleness and indecision—natural enough in extreme old age—which prevented Mr. Carlyle from making up his mind conclusively as to what he wished to be done about his papers, and having his decision put into writing. The paralysis which latterly disabled his hand from writing was no doubt a partial explanation of this. His sending his papers to you was inconclusive; whatever he said to Mrs. Alexander Carlyle in 1875 was inconclusive; so much so that she seems not to have appreciated its importance till her friends pointed it out to her some months after his death, and after she had conveyed a totally different impression to my mind of the state of affairs. Lastly, the conversations about the profits of the 'Reminiscences' were even more inconclusive and difficult to ascertain precisely than the rest. This, however, was no fault of his. The natural result of leaving such matters in such an ill-defined position was to cause the difficulties which subsequently arose.

I should like to add one further remark. People will of course differ as to the way in which you exercised the most painful discretion which Mr. Carlyle, in order to save himself the pain of a decision which he wished you to make for him, chose to impose upon you. I can bear testimony which throws light on the motives which influenced you in writing as you did. I believe them to be stated with absolute truth in your prefaces to the first volume of each of the two parts of his biography, and in a few words in a letter to Mr. Farrer of May 12, 1881, which I think he must have sent to Mrs. A. Carlyle: 'Carlyle's memory is as dear to me as it can possibly be to Mrs. A. Carlyle. I honoured and loved him above all men that I ever knew or shall know. It is my duty to show him as he was, and no life known to me, taken as a whole, will bear a more severe scrutiny. But he wished, especially wished, his faults to be known. They are nothing, amount to nothing, in the great balance of his qualities. But such as they were they must be described. Surely this is no unfriendly hand.' I believe this to be the truth, the whole truth, and nothing but the truth.

For about fifteen years I was the intimate friend and constant companion of both of you, and never in my life did I see any one man so much devoted to any other as you were to him during the whole of that period of time. The most affectionate son could not have acted better to the most venerated father. You cared for him, soothed him, protected him as a guide might protect a weak old man down a steep and painful path. The admiration you habitually expressed for him both morally and intellectually was unqualified. You never said to me one ill-natured word about him down to this day. It is to me wholly incredible that anything but a severe regard for truth, learnt to a great extent from his teaching, could ever have led you to embody in your portrait of him a delineation of the faults and weaknesses which mixed with his great qualities.

Of him I will make only one remark in justice to you. He did not use you well. He threw upon you the responsibility of a decision which he ought to have taken himself in a plain unmistakable way. He considered himself bound to expiate the wrongs which he had done to his wife. If he had done this himself it would have been a courageous thing; but he did not do it himself. He did not even decide for himself that it should be done after his death. If any courage was shown in the matter, it was shown by you, and not by him. You took the responsibility of deciding for him that it ought to be done. You took the odium of doing it, of avowing to the world the faults and weaknesses of one whom you regarded as your teacher and master. In order to present to the world a true picture of him as he really was, you, well knowing what you were about, stepped into a pillory in which you were charged with treachery, violation of confidence, and every imaginable base motive, when you were in fact guilty of no other fault than that of practising Mr. Carlyle's great doctrine that men ought to tell the truth.

Make any use you like of this, and give it any degree of publicity which you think desirable.

I am ever, my dear Froude,
Most sincerely yours,
J. F. STEPHEN.

APPENDIX.

Passages omitted from pp. 31 and 34, dealing with the publication of the 'Reminiscences' in the United States, and a claim to the literary profits of that book preferred by Mrs. A. Carlyle.

A SINGULAR fatality has attended me from first to last in this business, which has cost me so dear. I call it fatality. It was rather my own uncertainty of the road that I ought to follow which has left me exposed to so many accidents. I have now to mention a small collateral matter, insignificant in itself, but important from the consequences to which it led. It became known that Carlyle had written fragments of an autobiography, and that they were to be edited by me. An American friend, Mr. X., said to me one day that to his knowledge an American publisher, Mr. ——, would give an 'immense sum' for the right of bringing out such a volume in the United States if Carlyle would edit it himself, that Mr. —— had been Mr. Carlyle's American publisher, and had a right to the preference. He ought to have told me at the same time that he was Mr. ——'s agent in England, which I never suspected. He never named any particular sum except that it would be excessive and unusual. He spoke to me merely as a friend, and as a preliminary as I supposed, to a formal negotiation. I did not like his interference. Messrs. Scribner had been my own publishers in America, and I had always found them liberal and satisfactory. But as I supposed that a very large price indeed would be forthcoming I thought myself bound to tell Carlyle what Mr. X. had said. He replied at once that Mr. —— was no publisher of his, that to his knowledge he had never had anything to do with Mr. ——; but he did for a time think it possible that he might undertake the editing. He wished to do it, but on reflection he found it would try him too much. He turned it over to me. I must do it, he said, and he must be troubled no more about the matter. He only added that the book had better be brought out as soon as possible after his death. People would then be talking about him, and they would have something authentic to go upon. Mr. X. still advised that Mr. —— should bring the book out, giving as his opinion that the very large sum would still be forthcoming. I believed him. I said if that was so I was ready to make an agreement. I expected to hear from Mr. —— more particularly and directly. Meanwhile I did not think it could be right of me to keep a large sum of money for myself, coming as it did from Carlyle's work. That it would be mine legally I never doubted; but I told Mary Carlyle that I would give it to her. Carlyle himself never said a word to me on the subject, nor I to him. So far as I was concerned it was a spontaneous resolution of my own, and one which no one at all had a right to expect me to make. Mary Carlyle certainly did not think at the time that she had any claim to the profits of the 'Reminiscences.' She said when I mentioned the matter to her, as I think she must recollect, that all that would be mine. She had no pretension to it. I said, to make it easy for her to take a present from me, that she had more right to it than I; that the book would be Carlyle's, not mine; that she had worked hard for him, &c., &c. She said it was very generous of me. It appeared afterwards that she had misunderstood me, so far that she thought I was speaking of all the profits, English as well as American. I had not considered the English profits. I had merely in my mind the 'immense sum' of which X. had vaguely spoken. Possibly I was not sufficiently explicit. But, at any rate, if Mary Carlyle then supposed that she had any legal right she ought to have said so.

* * * * * * * *

I had waited in vain to hear more particularly about the immense sum from Mr. ——. From himself, or as far as I knew from any accredited agent of his, I had received no communication at all; and as time went on and nothing came from Mr. ——, and no specific sum at all was named, I dismissed the matter from my mind. I thought it had been some unauthorised notion of X.'s or that Mr. —— finding that Carlyle was not to edit the book had ceased to concern himself about it. I had made arrangements with my usual publisher, Mr. Scribner, and the book was in print in America as well as England, and was on the point of appearing when it came out that X. had all along been Mr. ——'s formal representative, that he had informed Mr. —— that I had promised the book to him—that I was bound by an engagement, as if I could be bound to anything before any terms had been specified. Mr. —— would undoubtedly publish a rival edition and the anticipated profits would come to nothing. The 'immense sum,' the amount of which I then learnt for the first time, was to have been a mere bagatelle, which had it been mentioned at first would have saved me from any difficulty or uncertainty, but it became too patent to me now, that the American profits would not amount at most to a tenth of what X. had led me vaguely to look for. It was nothing to me, but I had raised Mary Carlyle's expectations, and I had to consider what I would do. In fact, I was considering seriously the question of the profits of the book altogether. The undertaking itself had been a serious sacrifice, and, so far as money was concerned, I was likely to have made a bad bargain for myself if I had kept all. The 'Biography,' as it was now to be written, I was well aware could never be a popular one. Still there would be a certain sale. I was unwilling to lie under a shadow of suspicion that I had any pecuniary interests in a publication for which half the world would inevitably cry out upon me. I had decided to give Mary Carlyle, in addition to such profits on the 'Reminiscences' as might still come from America, half the English profits besides, and I had meant to give her half the profits of the 'Biography' as well, if I lived to write it. From this point of view at least I thought that no fault could be found with me. I even looked on myself as acting generously. To my extreme surprise, Mary Carlyle insisted that I had promised her the whole profits of the 'Reminiscences,' English and American. She refused to take less. She put herself into the hands of lawyers and commenced legal proceedings against me. At first she laid her claim upon my promise only—a strange enough proceeding save if she had no other. I explained to her what that promise had been. She would not believe, and accused me virtually of lying and trying to cheat her. Afterwards, when the world was open-mouthed upon me about the 'Reminiscences,' she refused to take any money at all from me, expecting, I suppose, to get it otherwise. She insisted that the manuscripts were hers, that they had been given to her by her uncle. She put in a claim no longer resting on my promise, but on an independent right of her own. She had taken down my own incautious words when I first mentioned the subject: that she had a better right to the money than I had, that the book was her uncle's writing, not mine, and she actually made it a part of her case. I was much astonished at all this. Not a doubt had ever crossed my mind that so far as legal right was concerned the money was my own, to keep or give away as I pleased, and I thought that I had been behaving liberally. To whom the manuscripts belonged was uncertain, but I had unquestionably the use of them for the composition of the 'Biography.' Mary Carlyle now said that they had long since been given to her. If so, I ought to have been told of it; as in that case I had been left for more than six years in possession of another person's property with directions to destroy what I pleased of it. Besides my literary duties in the matter, I was one of Carlyle's executors and had to act in a double capacity. My own offer and my own incautious words about it were being made the basis of a lawsuit against me which would and must involve my whole position as Carlyle's biographer. I had no wish to keep the money; I supposed that really I had not been distinct enough in what I had said about the American profits, and that she had in fact misunderstood me. In the storm that was raging I did not wish to have any fresh troubles about me. She was holding me literally to the words of my promise as she had understood it. I accepted her account. It had reference only to two-thirds of the book. For the 'Memoir' of Mrs. Carlyle was an addition to the original plan, and that was my own by her uncle's special bequest. The English profits of the book were 1,700*l*. Another 100*l*. had come from America. Of this 1,800*l*., 600*l*., even according to her own view, was strictly mine; of this 600*l*. I proposed to give her half, keeping but 300*l*. for myself. She told her lawyer that she would take nothing at all if she was to take it from me. I

deposited 1,500*l*. (to which I afterwards added as further
American profits about 130*l*.) with Mr. Carlyle's lawyers,
that when she pleased she might take it, or that she might
go to a court of law to recover it as her own. I, for my
own part, was now anxious that a court of law should be
appealed to. I should see my way as executor, and in my
own capacity I should be delivered out of complications
which threatened to choke me. Either the papers would
be declared to belong to me, or to belong to the executors,
or to belong to Mary Carlyle. If they belonged to me or
to the executors, I could go on peaceably with my work, so
far as I could have peace at all amidst the world's out-
cries. If to her, I should be delivered altogether from
further trouble about the matter. I should have lost ten
years of labour and anxiety, but I was ready to sacrifice
anything to escape out of a situation which was intolerable.
I would not then, I would not now, if I could help it, tell
the whole truth about Carlyle. If I had, the world would
at any rate have comprehended how I was situated, and
why I was acting as I did. I had more than once resolved to throw the work up and go no farther, but I had
promised Carlyle to write his 'Life,' and I did not like to
have my commission wrenched out of my hands by pre-
tensions which had not been proved to have a foundation.
A court of law would settle all that. The intricacies of
the situation would be disentangled under cross-examina-
tion, and we should all know where we stood. If Mary
Carlyle did not press her own claim, I wished to appeal
myself to the Court of Chancery to interpret Carlyle's will
and determine our several rights and duties. I was over-
ruled by my brother-executor, who was unwilling that
Carlyle's name should be soiled in a lawsuit. I have no
doubt that on the whole Sir James Stephen was right in
this. I had myself been worried into too great impatience.

At any rate, I submitted to his opinion. Mary Carlyle might do as she pleased. I left the money in Mr. Carlyle's solicitor's hands, that she might take it when she liked. I did not insist that she should acknowledge that she took it from me as a present. A tedious correspondence followed, with no issue save a long lawyer's bill for myself, which I confess I thought a most needless aggravation. In the end I believe Mary Carlyle was advised that the result of a lawsuit would be uncertain, and after long hesitation she took the money. I do her the justice to say that she never thanked me for it. She received it assuming it to be her own, and publicly denied that I had given her anything; 300*l.* of what she had was mine under any aspect of the matter. But I will say no more of this sordid aggravation of a situation which from the first had been anxious and now had become detestable. Of course she acted on high motives; she regarded herself as the protector of her uncle's reputation, which she considered me to have injured and to be injuring.

WILL AND CODICIL OF THOMAS CARLYLE, ESQ.

WILL dated 6th *February* 1873.
CODICIL dated 8th *November* 1878.

I THOMAS CARLYLE of 5 Great Cheyne Row Chelsea in the County of Middlesex Esquire declare this to be my last Will and Testament Revoking all former Wills. I DIRECT all my just debts funeral and testamentary expences to be paid as soon as may be after my decease AND it is my express instruction that since I cannot be laid in the Grave at Haddington I shall be placed beside my Father and Mother in the Churchyard of Ecclefechan I APPOINT my Brother JOHN AITKEN CARLYLE Doctor of Medicine and my Friend JOHN FORSTER of Palace Gate House Kensington Esquire Executors and Trustees of this my Will If my said Brother should die in my lifetime I APPOINT my Brother JAMES CARLYLE to be an EXECUTOR and TRUSTEE in his stead and if the said JOHN FORSTER should die in my lifetime I APPOINT my friend JAMES ANTHONY FROUDE to be an EXECUTOR and TRUSTEE in his stead I GIVE to my dear and ever helpful Brother JOHN. A. CARLYLE my Leasehold messuage in Great Cheyne Row in which I reside subject to the rent and covenants under which I hold the same and all such of my Furniture plate linen, china, books prints pictures and other effects therein as are not hereinafter bequeathed specifically. My Brother John has no need of my money or help, and therefore in addition to this small remembrance I BEQUEATH to him only the charge of being Executor of my Will and of seeing everything peaceably fulfilled. If he survives me, as is natural, he will not refuse My poor and indeed almost pathetic collection of books (with the exception of those hereinafter specifically given) I request him to accept as a memento of me while he stays behind I GIVE my Watch to my Nephew Thomas the son of my Brother Alexander, "Alick's Tom" as a Memorial of the affection I have for him and of my thankful (and also hopeful) approval of all that I have ever got to know or surmise about him He can understand that of all my outward possessions this Watch is become the dearest to me. It was given me on my Wedding by one who was herself invaluable to me; It had been her Father's. made to her Father's order; and had measured out into still more perfect punctuality his noble years of well-spent time; and now it has measured out (always punctually, it) nearly forty-seven years of mine, and still measures, as with an everloving solemnity, till time quite end with me: and may the new Thomas Carlyle fare not worse with it than his two predecessors have done. To Maggie Welsh my dear Cousin (and Hers) One hundred pounds. To my House servant Mrs. Warren if in my service at the time of my decease Fifty pounds. Having with good reason, ever since my first appearance in Literature, a variety of kind feelings obligations and regards towards New England, and indeed long before that a hearty good will, real and steady, which still continues, to America at large, and recognising with gratitude how much of friendliness, of actually credible human love, I have had from that Country, and what immensities of worth and capability I believe and partly know to be lodged, especially in the silent classes there, I have now after due consultation as to the feasibilities, the excusabilities of it, decided to fulfil a fond notion that has been hovering in my mind these many years; and I do therefore hereby bequeath the books, (whatever of them I could not borrow, but had to buy and gather, that is, in general whatever of them are still here) which I used in writing on Cromwell and Friedrich and which shall be accurately searched for, and parted from my other books, to the President and Fellows of Harvard College, City of Cambridge, State of Massachusetts, as a poor testimony of my respect for that alma mater of so many of my Trans-Atlantic friends, and a token of the feelings above indicated towards the Great Country of which Harvard is the Chief School, In which sense I have reason to be confident that the Harvard authorities will please to accept this my little bequest and deal with it, and order and use it, as to their own good judgment and kind fidelity shall seem fittest. A certain symbolical value the bequest may have, but of intrinsic value as a collection of old books it can pretend to very little. If there should be doubt as to any books coming within the category of this bequest my dear Brother John if left behind me, as I always trust and hope who already knows about this Harvard matter and who possesses a Catalogue or List drawn up by me of which the Counterpart is in possession of the Harvard Authorities, will see it for me in all points accurately done. In regard to this and to all else in these final directions of mine I wish him to be regarded as my Second Self, my Surviving Self. My manuscript entitled "Letters and Memorials of Jane Welsh Carlyle" is to me naturally, in my now bereaved state, of endless value, though of what value to others I cannot in the least clearly judge ; and indeed for the last four years am imperatively forbidden to write farther on it, or even to look farther into it. Of that manuscript my kind considerate and ever faithful friend James Anthony Froude (as he has lovingly promised me) takes precious charge in my stead. To him therefore I give it with whatever other fartherances and elucidations may be possible, and I solemnly request of him to do his best and wisest in the matter, as I feel assured he will.

There is incidentally a quantity of Autobiographic Record in my notes to this Manuscript ; but except as subsidiary and elucidative of the text I put no value on such. Express biography of me I had really rather that there should be none. James Anthony Froude John Forster and my Brother John, will make earnest survey of the Manuscript and its subsidiaries there or elsewhere, in respect to this as well as to its other bearings ; their united utmost candour and impartiality. taking always James Anthony Froude's practicality along with it. will evidently furnish a better judgment than mine can be. The Manuscript is by no means ready for publication ; nay the questions How, when (after what delay, seven ten years) it, or any portion of it, should be published, are still dark to me ; but on all such points James Anthony Froude's practical summing up and decision is to be taken as mine. The imperfect Copy of the said Manuscript which is among my papers with the original letters I give to my Niece Mary Carlyle Aitken, to whom also dear little soul, I bequeath Five hundred pounds for the loving care and unwearied patience and helpfulness she has shown to me in these my last solitary and infirm years. To her also I give at her choice, whatever Memorials of my Dear Departed One she has seen me silently preserving here, especially the table in the Drawing-Room at which I now write and the little Child's Chair (in the China Closet) which latter to my eyes has always a brightness as of Time's Morning and a sadness as of Death and Eternity when I look on it; and which, with the other dear Article, I have the weak wish to preserve in loving hands yet awhile when I am gone. My other Manuscripts I leave to my Brother John. They are with one exception of no moment to me. I have never seen any of them since they were written. One of them is a set of fragments about James First which were loyally fished out for me from much other Cromwellian rubbish, and doubtless carefully copied more than twenty years ago by the late John Chorley who was always so good to me. But neither this latter nor perhaps any of the others is worth printing. On this point however my Brother can take Counsel with John Forster and James Anthony Froude and do what is then judged fittest. Many or most of these papers I often feel that I myself should burn; but probably I never shall after all. The " one exception " spoken of above is a sketch of my Father and his life hastily thrown off in the nights between his death and burial, full of earnest affection and veracity, most likely unfit for printing; but I wish it to be taken charge of by my Brother John and preserved in the Family. Since, I think, the very night of my Father's Funeral (far away from London and me) I have never seen a word of that poor bit of writing. In regard to all business matters about my Books (of which not only the Copyrights but all the Stereotype plates from which the three several collected Editions have been respectively printed and which are at present deposited with my Printers Messrs. Robson and Son belong exclusively to me) Copyrights, Editions, and dealings with Booksellers and others in relation thereto. John Forster's advice is to be taken as supreme and complete, better than my own ever could have been. His faithful, wise, and ever punctual care about all that has been a miracle of generous helpfulness, literally invaluable to me in that field of things. Thanks, poor thanks, are all that I can return, alas! I GIVE the residue of my personal estate to my Trustees before named, In trust to convert into money such part of my Estate as shall not consist of money or securities for money, and Upon trust to invest in such securities as they shall think fit the moneys to arise from such conversion and the moneys and securities of which my personal Estate shall consist at the time of my decease: With power to change investments from time to time And to stand possessed thereof In trust as to one-fifth part thereof for my Brother Alexander absolutely And as to one-fifth part In trust for my Brother James absolutely And as to one other fifth part thereof In trust for my Sister Mary Wife of James Austin, farmer at Gill Cummertrees, Dumfriesshire absolutely for her separate use independent of the debts control or engagements of her present or any future Husband And as to one other fifth part thereof In trust for my Sister, Jean, the Wife of James Aitken of Dumfries absolutely for her separate use independent of the debts control or engagements of her present or any future husband. And as to the remaining fifth part thereof In trust for my Sister Janet, Wife of Robert Hanning of Hamilton Canada, absolutely, for her separate use independent of the debts control or engagements of her present or any future husband PROVIDED ALWAYS that if my said Brothers Alexander and James or my said Sisters or any or either of them shall die in my lifetime, the share or shares of him her or them so dying shall be In trust for the Children of my Brothers or Sisters respectively so dying who shall attain the age of Twenty-one years or being Daughters shall marry in equal shares but if there shall be no such Child then such share or shares shall go to the others or other of my said Brothers and Sisters in equal shares but so that the shares which may thus accrue to my Sisters shall be for their separate use in the same manner as their original shares. I direct all legacies to be paid free of duty I DIRECT that notwithstanding the trust for conversion hereinbefore contained my Trustees shall have absolute authority to postpone the conversion for any period not exceeding two years after my death of all or any part of my personal estate and I say this with especial reference to my Copyrights. And the income to be derived from my Estate previous to its conversion shall be applied in the same way as the income of my estate if converted would be applicable To my dear friends John Forster and James Anthony Froude (Masson too I should remember in this moment and perhaps some others) I have nothing to leave that could be in the least worthy of them but if they, or any of them, could find among my reliques a Memorial they would like, who of Men could deserve it better. No Man at this time. If no such choice be made by themselves I leave to Forster Faithornes Print of Cromwell between the Pillars, now in the Drawing Room here, and to Froude Pesne's Portrait of Wilhelmina with the Fontange on her brow, now in the same Room. **In witness** whereof I the said Thomas Carlyle the Testator have to this my last Will and Testament set my hand this sixth day of February One thousand eight hundred and seventy-three.

Signed and DECLARED by the said Thomas Carlyle the Testator as and for his last Will and Testament in the presence of us both present at the same time who in his presence at his request and in the presence of each other hereunto subscribe our names as Witnesses.
} T. CARLYLE

    WILLIAM HARES
        Butler
                Palace Gate House

    FREDERIC OUVRY
            66 Lincoln's Inn Fields Solicitor.

This IS A CODICIL to the last Will and Testament of me THOMAS CARLYLE of No. 24 Cheyne Row Chelsea in the County of Middlesex Esquire which said Will bears date the Sixth day of February One thousand eight hundred and seventy-three WHEREAS by my said Will I have appointed my Brother JOHN AITKEN CARLYLE Doctor of Medicine and JOHN FORSTER Esquire Executors and Trustees thereof and appointed and directed that if my said Brother should die in my lifetime my Brother JAMES CARLYLE should be an Executor and Trustee in his stead And that if the said JOHN FORSTER should die in my lifetime my friend JAMES ANTHONY FROUDE should be an Executor and Trustee in his stead AND WHEREAS my dear and ever faithful friend the said JOHN FORSTER has been taken from me by death and I am desirous of revoking the said appointment of Executors and Trustees contained in my said Will and of appointing my said Brother JOHN AITKEN CARLYLE the said JAMES ANTHONY FROUDE and Sir JAMES FITZJAMES STEPHEN of No. 24 Cornwall Gardens South Kensington in the said County of Middlesex K.C.S.I Q.C. to be Executors and Trustees of my said Will Now THEREFORE I do hereby revoke the above recited appointment of Executors and Trustees contained in my said Will and do hereby appoint my said Brother JOHN AITKEN CARLYLE the said JAMES ANTHONY FROUDE and the said Sir JAMES FITZJAMES STEPHEN to be Executors and Trustees of my said Will I HEREBY REVOKE the gift in my said Will of the Writing table belonging to me which stands in the Drawing Room at No. 24 Cheyne Row aforesaid and hereby give and bequeath the same writing table to the said Sir James FitzJames Stephen I know he will accept it as a distinguished mark of my esteem He knows that it belonged to my honoured Father in Law and his daughter And that I have written all my Books upon it except only Schiller and that for the fifty years and upwards that are now past I have considered it among the most precious of my possessions I GIVE and BEQUEATH the Screen which stands in the Drawing Room at No. 24 Cheyne Row aforesaid to my dear Niece Mary Carlyle Aitken who best knows the value I have always put upon it and will best take care of it to the end

of her life when I am gone She knows by whom it was
made and I wish her to accept it as a testimony of the
trust I repose in her and as a mark of my esteem for her
honourable veracious and faithful character and a memorial
of all the kind and ever faithful service she has done me
The Faithorne Portrait of Oliver Cromwell which I had
intended for my loving and ever faithful friend John
Forster the only bequest he would accept of from me I
now give and bequeath to his Widow Mrs. Forster and I
beg her to accept it in memory of him and of me I GIVE
and BEQUEATH to my dear friend David Masson my photo-
graphically printed folio copy of Shakespeare's Works in
memory of me The two pictures of Luther's Father and
Mother which were a gift to me from Mr. Robert Tait of
Queen Anne Street Cavendish Square in the said County of
Middlesex I give back to him The large oil painting which
hangs in the Drawing room at No. 24 Cheyne Row aforesaid and which has been engraved under the title of " The
little Drummer " I give and bequeath to Louisa Caroline
the Dowager Lady Ashburton for her life and after her
death to her Daughter The Honorable Mary Florence
Baring absolutely AND WHEREAS by my said Will I have
given to my said dear Brother John Aitken Carlyle my
Leasehold messuage No. 24 Cheyne Row aforesaid in which
I reside subject to the rent and covenants under which I
hold the same and all such of my Furniture plate china
linen books prints pictures and other effects therein as are
not by my said Will bequeathed specifically AND WHEREAS
I am desirous of revoking such gift and of making such
bequest of the said messuage property and effects as hereinafter appears Now THEREFORE I do hereby revoke the
said gift of the said messuage property and effects and
hereby bequeath the said last mentioned leasehold messuage and all such of my Furniture plate linen china books
prints pictures and other effects therein as are not by my

said Will and this my Codicil bequeathed specifically unto my said Brother John Aitken Carlyle for his life he paying the rent and all rates taxes and outgoings payable in respect of the same messuage and performing the covenants and conditions under which I hold the same and after his death I give and bequeath the same messuage furniture plate linen china books prints pictures and other effects unto my said Niece Mary Carlyle Aitken absolutely In all other respects I confirm my said Will In witness whereof I have to this Codicil to my said Will set my hand this Eighth day of November One thousand eight hundred and seventy-eight

Signed and Declared by the said Thomas Carlyle the Testator as and for a Codicil to his last Will and Testament in the presence of us who in his presence at his request and in the presence of each other (both being present together at the same time) have hereunto subscribed our names as Witnesses.

T. CARLYLE

VICTOR H DEACON
Sol^r
C. ERNEST. BOWLES.

Clerks to Messrs. FARRER OUVRY & CO
Sol^{rs}
66 Lincoln's Inn Fields London